Trackers and T...
by Robin Shar[ples]
Illustrated by Simon Smith

> **Hello!**
> I'm Robin—you might have met me before in one of the other Livewires books. If you have read any of the others, I hope that you like them. I know that it doesn't take long to read all the adventures that the Livewires get into, but do remember to do the puzzles and fill in the diary pages. There is a diary page for every six adventure pages so you can turn the Livewires book into your own special adventure diary whenever you like. Have fun!

Text copyright © Robin Sharples 1997

Illustrations copyright © Simon Smith 1997

The author asserts the moral right to be identified as the author of this work.

Published by **The Bible Reading Fellowship**
Peter's Way, Sandy Lane West, Oxford OX4 5HG
ISBN 0 7459 3549 4

First edition 1997

10 9 8 7 6 5 4 3 2 1 0

All rights reserved

Acknowledgments
Unless otherwise stated, scripture quotations are taken from the Good News Bible published by The Bible Societies/HarperCollins Publishers Ltd UK © American Bible Society, 1966, 1971, 1976, 1992.

A catalogue record for this book is available from the British Library.

Printed and bound in Malta by Interprint Limited

Barnabas

An imprint of The Bible Reading Fellowship

Hi! I'm Data and this is us at my sleepover party. I love it when everyone comes round to our house. That's me relaxing with Quartz and listening to music. Quartz's twin brother, Digit, and my sister, Annie-log, are with Tim over by the computer—they had better watch out 'cos Boot, the computer, has a habit of going his own way when we're not looking. Little Ben seems to be too absorbed playing with Tempo to notice. Tempo's the little dog hiding behind the bed. We met him at the beginning of the Bible—you can read about that in the very first Livewires adventure.

When we have sleepovers we always try to stay awake as long as we can. All except Tempo, he goes to sleep as often as possible. Anyway, at this sleepover we were all talking when we heard a funny noise. It was Boot, Annie-log's computer, snoring; he's never been the same since we had a power cut. We carried on talking quietly as the night got colder and colder, and one by one we fell asleep...

The Livewires lay quietly in the cold of the night. Boot couldn't rest—he hated the cold. He finally fell asleep, but he whirred and clicked as he slumbered.

Suddenly the Livewires were woken by a freezing gust of wind. Boot's disk drive was whirring faster and faster and the Livewires found themselves caught up in a sleepy heap and whisked into the air.

WHOOSH!

Boot!

The advisers played a game in prison: they tried to make different words from the letters of Nebuchadnezzar—how many can you make?

NEBUCHADNEZZAR

It was about a great statue made of different things and it meant that there would be other kings and kingdoms after Nebuchadnezzar and that in the end God's kingdom would come and be greater than any of the others.

That's true, look what the Bible says about Daniel's words.

"The great God is telling Your Majesty what will happen in the future. I have told you exactly what you dreamt, and have given you its true meaning."

Your God is the greatest of all gods. Daniel, I shall give you your reward and a special job here at the royal court.

Daniel 2:45

So here I am, at the royal court and one of the most important people in the country!

Dear Father, I know that you are always there to watch over me. Please help me to feel you close when I feel frightened or alone. Amen.

Did you feel sorry for those advisers in prison? Daniel knew he could trust God, though. Is there a prayer that you like to say when you feel frightened or alone? You'll find one you could say in the prayer cloud.

Even if Nebuchadnezzar had learned his lesson, his family didn't...

The strangest thing that happened to me was at a feast when Belshazzar was king. Everyone was having a good time when . . .

MENE MENE TEKEL U-PHARSIN

A hand wrote on the wall . . . No one could read the words, so I was sent for . . .

I could see what it was all about right away, so I spoke to the king . . .

"You did not honour the God who determines whether you live or die and who controls everything you do. That is why God has sent the hand to write these words. This is what was written: Number, number, weight, divisions."

Daniel 5:23

Daniel went on to explain that the words were like a clue to a picture.

God had weighed the work of the king and found that it was not complete or good, so God had counted the number of days that the king had left and was going to divide the kingdom up...

That very night Belshazzar died and Darius became king. He was from a land called Media, north east of Babylon.

Digit wrote something on his pad . . . Can you understand it?

8

This is terrible. I can't sleep, I can't eat. I do hope that Daniel is all right.

The Livewires saw Darius slip out of the palace before it got light. They followed him...

Daniel! Daniel!

Has he gone mad too?

No, look he is shouting into that hole.

It must be the lion's pit!

Daniel! Daniel!

Oh no, there is no reply. Daniel must be...

No, listen...

May Your Majesty live for ever. God sent his angel to shut the mouths of the lions so that they would not hurt me...

I command that throughout my empire everyone should fear and respect Daniel's God.

He is a living God, and he will rule for ever. His kingdom will never be destroyed, and his power will never come to an end. He saves and rescues; he performs wonders and miracles in heaven and on earth. He saved Daniel from being killed by the lions.

Daniel 6:26

God is using Daniel to train the kings to look to God for strength and power, not those tricky advisers.

So, we're tracking the trainer! Come on, let's go and see Daniel.

Data has been using her compass a lot in this adventure. Can you track round it from north back to north, visiting east, south and west on the way—without crossing or using the same paths!

DIARY

SUNDAY
Do you remember your last dream?

MONDAY
What would be your 'dream come true'?

TUESDAY
Is Jerusalem west of your house? Perhaps you could ask someone to help you find out.

WEDNESDAY
How many words did you make from 'Nebuchadnezzar'?

THURSDAY
What were the names of the three kings Daniel mentioned?

FRIDAY
Send some messages to your friend using a code like Digit's. You could make up your own...

SATURDAY
My prayer to end the week would be:

The code Digit used is this one...
Can you read the message he wrote now?

How come he still can't tell the difference between a mouse and a rat?

Well, at least he spoke to you. Dogs don't seem very welcome in Babylon...

Why do you pray so much Daniel, even when you might get into trouble? **Because of the things that God has done for his people and what happened when God's people stopped praying to their God and worshipped the false gods of people around them...**

They stopped worshipping the Lord, the God of their ancestors, the God who had brought them out of Egypt, and they began to worship other gods, the gods of the peoples round them. And so the Lord became furious with Israel and let raiders attack and rob them, and the Israelites could no longer protect themselves.

Where's that from, Boot?

Judges 2: 12 & 14

It's from one of our old books, the book of Judges. Your window is very clever to know that.

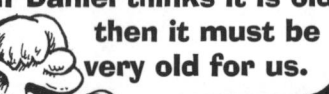

But what does it mean?

It can't mean much. If Daniel thinks it is old then it must be very old for us.

No, it's older than that, it's probably very, very old.

It may be very, very, very old even...

Tell us how old, please Daniel —or these two will go on talking rubbish all day!

Well I don't know exactly, but it could be over 700 years ago.

The stories that Daniel is talking about ARE very old! Let's do some maths!

If Daniel lived about 2,300 years ago and the book of Judges was written about 700 years before Daniel, how long ago was the book of Judges written?

3,000 yrs

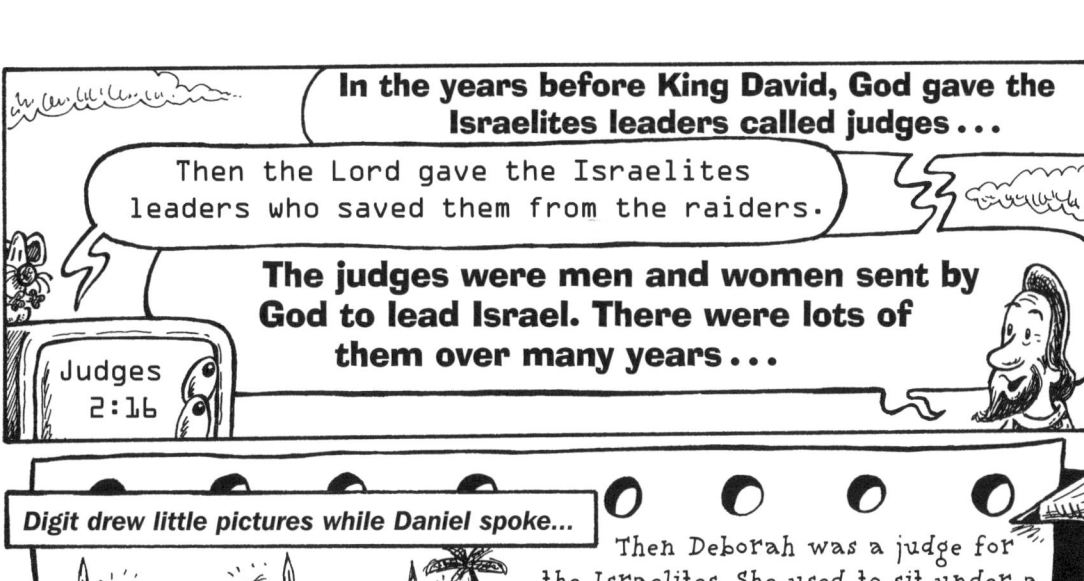

In the years before King David, God gave the Israelites leaders called judges...

Then the Lord gave the Israelites leaders who saved them from the raiders.

Judges 2:16

The judges were men and women sent by God to lead Israel. There were lots of them over many years...

Digit drew little pictures while Daniel spoke...

Then Deborah was a judge for the Israelites. She used to sit under a palm tree and the people would go to her for advice... she won a battle too...

Othniel was the first judge to free the Israelites from the raiders...

Then came Ehud, who was left-handed— he won a battle...

Did they just fight battles then?

No, the judges led Israel in peace time too, but there were also battles against the raiders...

And Gideon, who also won a great battle...

And Jephthah, who was a brave soldier...

Daniel went on to explain that the Israelites did not always win because they did not always do the things which pleased God and that the judges were chosen by God to train the people to follow him and the laws that they had been given in the time of Moses and Aaron.

More trainers for us to track!

Daniel has explained that the book of Judges is very old. Here is a way of making some writing look very old.

13

First of all find a nice piece of paper, then soak it in some very strong tea or coffee. If you let it dry it will be brown. Now copy out some of the Bible onto it, or make up some writing of your own (you could even use a code!). It will look quite old when it is dry. To make it look even older you can bake it in the oven. Get an adult to help you and keep on checking it or it might burn and then it would be spoiled!

Gideon took a long time to believe that God would give him enough strength to defeat the Midianites.

Sometimes it isn't easy to believe that God is there giving us strength. Here is a prayer for those difficult times:

Father, sometimes it is easy to know you are there. Help us, when it is not so easy, to know that you still give us strength. Amen.

15

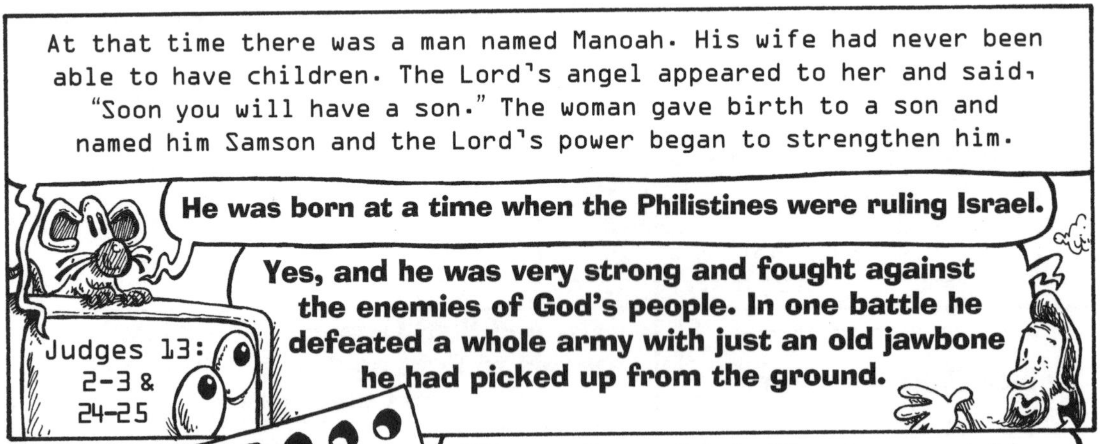

At that time there was a man named Manoah. His wife had never been able to have children. The Lord's angel appeared to her and said, "Soon you will have a son." The woman gave birth to a son and named him Samson and the Lord's power began to strengthen him.

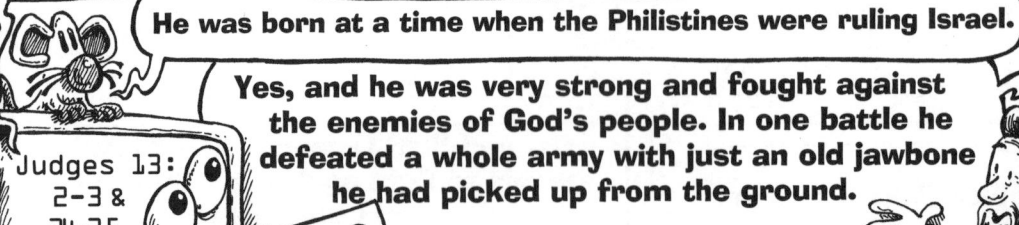

Judges 13: 2-3 & 24-25

There have been a lot of strange names in the stories that Daniel is telling. This wordsearch will remind you of them.

Samson, Deborah, Gideon, Ehud, Jephthah

```
A G S A M S O N Q
B I C D E D Q E R
F D E B O R A H P
J E P H T H A H M
O O K L E H U D B
M N N I S G R H G
```

No one wanted to meet Samson. He had a terrible temper and was not always good at keeping his promises.

Which promises did he break then...?

The most important one was about his promise to God.

What was that!!?

Well, one of Samson's promises was never to cut his hair. This is important really because it was a promise which showed he was obedient to God.

So why did he cut his hair?

He fell in love with a girl called Delilah. She was paid lots of money to find out what made Samson strong. He wouldn't tell her the truth at first, but...

First Samson told her to tie him up with strong ropes... but still he was strong.

Then he told her to weave his hair onto a loom and fix it with a tent peg... but still he was strong.

Finally he told her that if his hair was cut he would no longer be strong...

As soon as she cut his hair he was captured by the Philistines and taken captive. A little while after this the king wanted to show off, so he had Samson brought to his palace. He didn't think about the fact that Samson's hair had grown again! The king stood Samson in the middle of his palace to show him off, but Samson, sorry for all the silly things that he had done, prayed to God for strength, then pushed two pillars over and the whole building fell down!

17

DIARY

SUNDAY
Do you ever make promises?

MONDAY
Do you ever break promises?

TUESDAY
How do you remember your promises? Samson let his hair grow, the Egyptians used to shave their heads! What do you do?

WEDNESDAY
What makes you strong? Exercises? Breakfast cereal? Anything else...?

THURSDAY
Other than physical strength—what other ways are there of being strong?

FRIDAY
How can training help you feel stronger?

SATURDAY
Dear God, thank you for all the things that you have given me that keep me healthy and strong. Amen.

There was no king in Israel at that time. All the people did just as they pleased.
Judges 21:25

It's a bit like Data's compass, spinning round and not following any of the rules: Samson didn't follow the rules either.

Tim, sit down!

Tim didn't sit down, he went on spinning round and yelling until...

TIM!

18 *It was too late, Tim was dizzy. He tried to stop, but twisted round and fell over onto Boot. There was a whoosh and then silence.*

It's easy, we'll just type 'Daniel' and go back.

Do you know how many times Daniel's name is written in the Bible? What happens if we get the wrong place? We still wouldn't find Data.

Soon the Livewires were having a great argument about what they could do, all that is except Tychi and Boot...

The name 'Daniel' is in the Bible over forty times and it isn't even always the same person— they could end up anywhere!

The Livewires' arguing was ended by the sound of a horn blowing.

Wh..a...a..a..t!

It came from over there.

The Livewires crawled up a hill and looked down. There was a large tent. Behind it they could see a huge crowd of people busy putting up smaller tents of their own. Some of them had left their work and were walking to the big tent.

What is going on?

I saw something like this on telly, lots of people all camping together. They were called refugees, I think.

Where have they all come from?

Can you find two tents which are the same?

Quartz is right, these people are refugees escaping from slavery. If, like Quartz, you have seen anything like this on telly you might like to say this prayer:

Dear God, please be with all those people who have no home to go to and have to spend their days wandering. Be with them in their sadness and loneliness.
Amen.

19

A man came out of the big tent and sat in the shade outside it.

Look—we can't go and find Data until we have a plan. Let's start by finding out where we are. I'm going to ask that man.

Annie-log stood up and walked boldly down to the tent.

Excuse me! Can you tell me where we are?

Er, um. Shalom... I don't know!

What?

The man told them that his name was Aaron and that he was wandering through the desert with Moses and all the people of Israel.

The more he told them the more amazed the Livewires were. Aaron told them how he had been chosen by God to help Moses speak to the king of Egypt, and to help the people of Israel to escape from Egypt—you can read all about that in another Livewires adventure.

I went with Moses 'cos I can always think of something to say.

Like Digit!

Annie-log was puzzled by something...

Why is this tent so different from the others?

This is the tabernacle, the special tent where we worship God.

"For the entrance of the Tent make a curtain of fine linen woven with blue, purple, and red wool and decorated with embroidery."

Exodus 26:36

The tabernacle tent was big and colourful. You can read all about it in Exodus chapter 26—Exodus is the second book in the Bible, after Genesis.

You could colour this picture of the tabernacle tent.

20

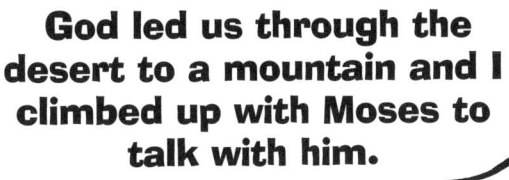

Aaron explained that there were all sorts of ways to remember the laws such as tying them on their hands and by putting tassels on their clothes.

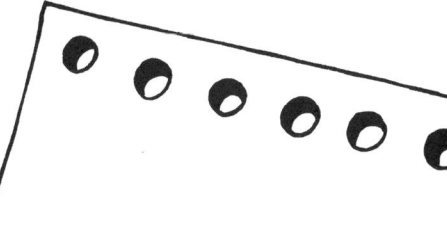

What important things do you have to remember?

What do you take to school?

What important things do you have to remember on days when you don't go to school? Write them on the sketchpad.

Boot beeped and his screen sprang to life.

> The people saw that Moses had not come down from the mountain. They gathered round Aaron and said to him, "We do not know what has happened to this man Moses, who led us out of Egypt; so make us a god to lead us."
>
> Exodus 32:1

Little Ben is right. Aaron should not have let the people persuade him to make a statue.

Dear Lord, please help us to always follow your rules, so that we will learn the things that you are training us for.

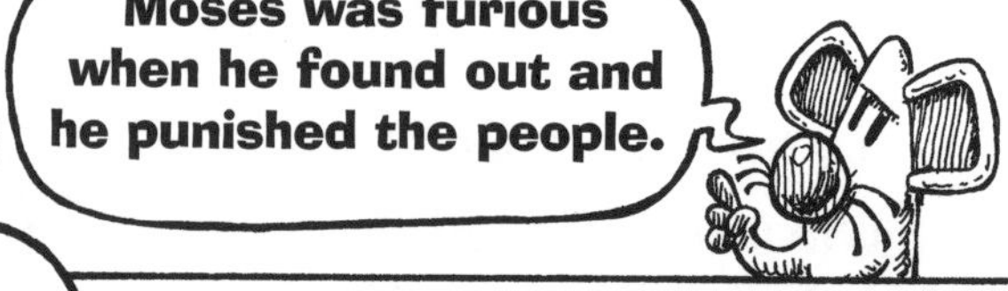

Have you ever let people persuade you to do things that you know you shouldn't do?

The Livewires spent the night in a little tent. During the night Little Ben thought he heard the horn again, but playing differently this time. He was too tired to bother about it, and he went back to sleep.

When the Livewires finally woke up the Israelites had gone!

"Where are they all?"

"What happened to Aaron?"

Annie-log rushed to Boot and typed furiously. Nothing happened.

Tychi crawled under her hand and she moved the pointer to 'search' on Boot's screen. She typed 'Aaron' and Boot burst into activity.

```
The Lord said to Moses, "Tell the
   people of Israel to give you
twelve sticks, one from the leader
   of each tribe. Write each man's
   name on his stick and then write
      Aaron's name on the stick
   representing Levi. Take them to
     the Tent of my presence and put
   them in front of the Covenant Box.
   Then the stick of
     the man I have
      chosen will
        sprout."
```

Numbers 17:1-5

"What was that all about?"

"I don't know, but it seems like Aaron is still being given a chance to be a leader of Israel even though he made lots of mistakes."

"My mum says we learn by our mistakes."

"That's it! Aaron is learning—he's being trained to be the leader of the priests."

"Like training for football. Do you think God will do a miracle to show that Aaron has been picked for the team?"

What do you think? Follow the tendrils to find out which stick has sprouted—and then decorate it with buds, blossom and almonds. (Look at Numbers 17 verse 8 to find out whose stick it was.)

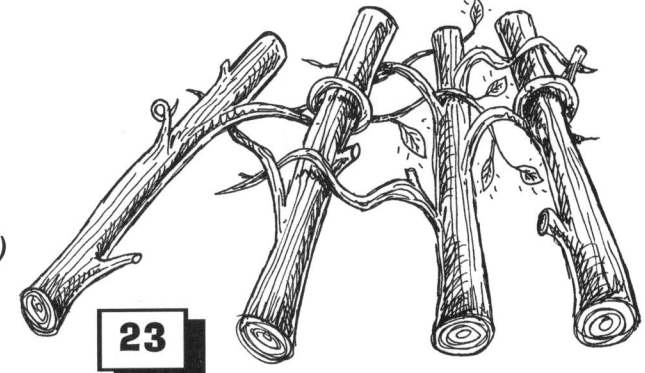

"It's great that Aaron was picked, but what happens when he can't do it any more?"

"I wonder if the ancient Israelites had training sessions for their leaders like we do for football."

"...and skating!"

"...and choir!"

"Of course they had training. It was done in the family. Aaron trained his son to carry on after him... mind you, I wish I could train Boot a little better."

"...so what happened when Aaron was too old to lead?"

Annie-log typed into Boot's keyboard. They didn't go anywhere this time, but Boot did show them the answer.

The Lord said, "Take Aaron and his son Eleazar up mount Hor, and there remove Aaron's priestly robes and put them on Eleazar." There on the top of the mountain Aaron died, and Moses and Eleazar came back down. The whole community learnt that Aaron had died, and they all mourned for him for 30 days.

24

Father God, we all try to follow you and learn your ways. Help us to listen to the people who train us, and help them to keep track of us so that when it is our turn to train or lead we will be ready. Amen

Numbers 20:23

So you see Tychi was right, Aaron's son did take over.

"Of course!"

DIARY

SUNDAY
Why do we need laws?

MONDAY
Which laws do you think are the most important?

TUESDAY
If you were making laws what would they say?

WEDNESDAY
What are God's laws called?

THURSDAY
How many of God's laws do you know?

FRIDAY
Look up Exodus 20 to see if you were right.

SATURDAY

> Father God, help me remember your laws! Amen.

Annie-log was looking very miserable...

What do we do about Data? She's with Daniel still, I suppose.

How about if Tempo finds her with his nose!

I know that I can smell well, but I can't smell that far!

Doesn't Boot have something clever to say about it?

Too right he does, he wouldn't let us down... I don't think!

Proverbs 27:10

```
Do not forget
your friends.
```

The Livewires knew that they could not forget Data completely, but they realized that they had not really remembered her when they were with Aaron.

Can you remember how the Israelites in the desert tried to remember God's laws?

They tied the laws to themselves...

They put tassels on their clothes...

Little Ben suddenly brightened up and took something from his pocket...

We can't forget Data, I've got her compass!

Father God, it is very easy for us to forget things. Help us remember that you don't forget and help us to try and remember too. Amen.

Have you ever forgotten a friend?

Have you forgotten someone's birthday?

How did you feel?

Mum trusted me to look after Data.

A tear trickled down Boot's screen and landed on one of his keys.

Keep safe what has been entrusted to your care.

Oh, Boot. So it IS all my fault!

Well, yes...

and no...

1 Timothy 6:20

Quartz and Digit were right. Annie-log's Mum had trusted her to look after Data.

But we were all there to help. We're all to blame for letting Data get lost.

Dear God, thank you for the people who are there for us when we need help. Help us to be there for others too. Amen.

Annie-log smiled tearfully at her friends—pleased they wanted to share the problem with her.

Ben went to sit with Annie-log.

We won't give up, Annie-log. Together we'll find Data.

Do you ever feel that you are left alone to sort out your problems?

Who would you ask to help?

Why?

The Livewires were helping Annie-log by trying to comfort her and share the blame, but she still didn't know how to solve the problem. Then Digit had a good idea...

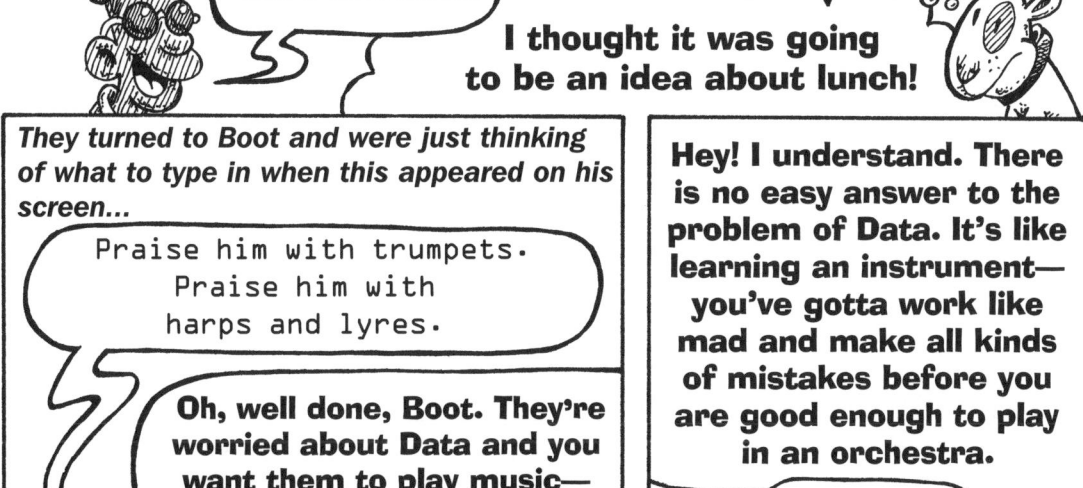

Boot had made the Livewires think. They realized that it didn't matter how many tries it took—something just had to be done until they were right.

Here's a game to play with your friends where you just have to keep on going until you get it right.

1. Ask a friend to think of a number.
2. Now you tell them a number.
3. They can only tell you if their number is greater than (>) less than (<) or equal to (=) your number
4. When your number is equal to theirs you win. Swap over and start again. (You can make this game easier by agreeing to use only numbers from 1 to 100 or 1 to 1000 if you like.)

SUNDAY
Still no sign of Data...

MONDAY
Still no sign of Data...

TUESDAY
18 tries and Tempo's fur is full of sand...

WEDNESDAY
The Livewires are getting tired...

THURSDAY
Still no sign of Data...

FRIDAY
Even Tychi is getting tired...

SATURDAY
36 tries...

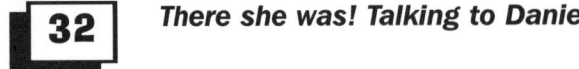
There she was! Talking to Daniel.

There you are. I've had a lovely time... nice food... a swim in the river... sun-bathing...

Well, we're glad that you enjoyed it!

What sorts of food are good for you? Which are bad?

Make a chart here

Good	Bad

Which do you like best, the good things or the bad ones?!!

God brings strength in all sorts of places and all sorts of ways—often in very surprising ways.

Boot knows a story about a man whose legs were so weak that he couldn't walk...

In Lystra there was a man who had been lame from birth and had never been able to walk. He sat there and listened to Paul's words. Paul saw that he believed and could be healed, so he looked straight at him and said in a loud voice, "Stand up straight on your feet!" The man jumped up and started walking around.

Acts 14: 8-10

That's a great story... I wonder if we'll get to meet this Paul bloke?

The Livewires could see that God brought strength, so Data suggested that they could pray at mealtimes as a reminder that it is God who gives us the food which helps to make us strong.

The Livewires decided to make a set of grace cards when they got back. If you find some pieces of card you'll be able to make them as well...

Dear Father God, thank you for all the things that make us strong, especially the food that you give to us. Help us to use it well and to share with those who have little.

I bet the instructions are on the diary page.

But there is more to strength than food or a trainer with a special sponge—as Tim suddenly realized...

But, don't we have to train as well, I mean like footballers do?

How do we train to have God's strength? That doesn't make sense!

Of course it does, it just takes a bit of practice. Show them what I mean, Boot...

Build up your strength with the Lord. Pray on every occasion. Pray always for all God's people.

Ephesians 6:10 & 18

Prayer!

That's what Daniel did...

...and Gideon...

...and Moses and Aaron.

I see! So whenever you pray you are training and building up your strength with God.

But praying is boring...

No it isn't! You can say all sorts of different kinds of prayer...

Annie-log is right. You can say 'thank you' prayers, 'sorry' prayers, 'please' prayers... How many different kinds of prayer can you think of? Make a note of them in the prayer cloud.

Don't forget to listen to what God is saying to you, too!

So if God is to look after us like our trainer does, what do we have to do?

What were those laws that Aaron told us about?

But that was ages ago, even before Jesus was born.

But Jesus knew those laws too, look...

Boot beeped, quite a lot. When the Livewires turned to him, he was ready with his screen.

John 13: 34 & 35

And now I give you a new commandment: love one another. If you have love for one another, everyone will know that you are my disciples.

38 To help you remember this make a piece of old paper (like you did when the Livewires were learning about the judges on page 13) and write the law in Boot's bubble on it.

Love one another

Then trace this diagram onto card to make a box. Decorate it before you make it up. Before you close it put Jesus' new commandment inside so that it is kept safe. Then every time you see it you will remember what to do to train for God.

DIARY

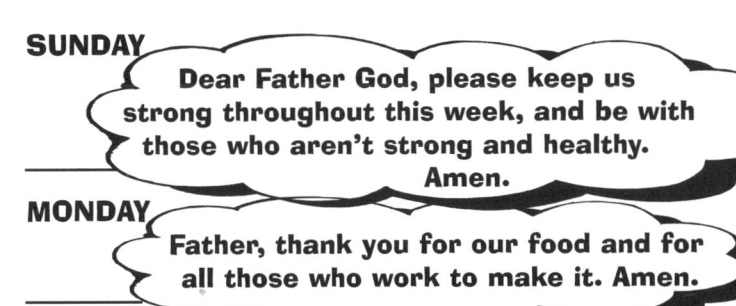

SUNDAY
Dear Father God, please keep us strong throughout this week, and be with those who aren't strong and healthy. Amen.

MONDAY
Father, thank you for our food and for all those who work to make it. Amen.

TUESDAY
Dear Lord, food is for all of us to share. As we eat, help us to remember all those people of the world who do not have enough food to keep them strong. Amen.

WEDNESDAY
Our Father, thank you for the friends whom we share our food with. Amen.

THURSDAY
Mighty God, as we eat our meals be with us and help us remember that it was you who made all the good things that we can taste. Amen.

FRIDAY
Lord God, thank you for my favourite food. Amen.

SATURDAY
Father, thank you for the people who prepared this food for us to eat. Amen.

Dogs have a special way of saying 'thank-you'—it's all in the tail!

Each of the days has a prayer. Copy these onto cards. Shuffle them together and then at the main meal of each day choose a card and read the grace. Then put that card aside until next week. If you make more than seven cards you get more choice!

The Livewires were still puzzled. How were they to follow these laws that Aaron had mentioned? How were they to learn the things that God wanted?

Data had a bright idea. She typed into Boot 'search' and 'trainer'.

Immediately they were whisked away...

The Livewires landed outside a house with white walls. Through a gate they could see a figure reading.

> He appeared in human form, was shown to be right by the Spirit, and was seen by angels. He was preached among the nations, was believed in throughout the world, and was taken up to heaven.
>
> 1 Timothy 3:16

"Where is that from, Boot?"

"What's he reading?"

"Looks like a letter."

"Let's go and say hello."

"No, he might be cross."

"Tempo! Come back!"

"Woof!"

It was too late. Tempo ran through the gate and into the garden. The Livewires had no choice but to follow him. The gate was locked, but the man reading the letter came to it when he saw them. He had a key...

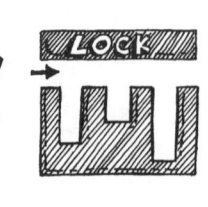

Which key fits the lock?

40

Er... hello, sorry about the dog!

Oh, who are you?

The Livewires!

What are Livewires?

It's our gang, we're cool!

Well, move into the sun...

No, that's not what Quartz means. Who are you?

I'm Timothy...

C-o-o-o-l—that's me...

It isn't cool in the sun, come out here...

Shut up, Tim. Sorry, which Timothy are you?

What do you mean?

Well, in our Bible there are two Timothys. 1 Timothy and 2 Timothy. Someone called Paul wrote to them. Tell him, Boot.

Paul travelled on to Derbe and Lystra, where a Christian named Timothy lived. His mother, who was also a Christian, was Jewish, but his father was a Greek. All the believers in Lystra and Iconium spoke well of Timothy.

Acts 16:1

HA HA HA

Timothy stared at Boot in surprise... and then he began to laugh. Do you know why he's laughing?

"I spent a lot of time with Paul until he was arrested. I think he is in Rome now—he's written this letter to me. I don't know about the other letter. I went around with him and his friends Silas, Luke and Barnabas. Paul is very good to me; I know he sometimes loses his temper, but then nobody is quite perfect are they?"

"Boot thinks he is! I have to keep him under control."

"I remember when we were in a place called Thessalonica. There were many Jews there who were angry with the things that Paul was saying about Jesus."

Acts 17:5

"Some Jews were jealous and formed a mob. They set the whole city in an uproar and attacked the home of a man called Jason in an attempt to find Paul and Silas."

"Why would they do that?"

42

Timothy explained that some of the Jews thought that the Christians were saying terrible things about God—they called it blasphemy. Timothy said that the Christians did not really mean them any harm.

"Did they find Paul?"

"No. We all had to escape during the night. It was quite exciting running through the streets in the darkness. We escaped to a town called Berea. I stayed there for a while teaching and learning more about Jesus."

"Father, help us to carry on following Jesus and help us to keep tracking you—even when we feel we're running through the dark! Amen."

Following Jesus isn't always easy, as Timothy found out...

We met many kind people on our travels. One was a lady called Lydia. She gave us a place to sleep when we stayed in the town of Philippi.

In Philippi we found ourselves in trouble and were thrown into prison! This was because many of the traders were angry with us because Paul had healed a girl who the traders were using as a slave. She could tell the future, but when Paul healed her she couldn't do it any more. Paul and his friend Silas were arrested and thrown into prison.

Prison can't keep God out, can it Boot?

About midnight Paul and Silas were praying and singing hymns to God, and the other prisoners were listening to them. Suddenly there was a violent earthquake, which shook the prison to its foundations. At once all the doors opened, and the chains fell off all the prisoners.

Acts 16:25-26

The Livewires were amazed...

Wow!

That's true, but Paul didn't run away. He and Silas stayed in the prison till the morning when they were let out anyway! Paul was cross because he and Silas had been punished for no reason—and they were Roman citizens too.

God did not forget Paul even in prison. Make this special box to remind you that even in the most difficult places God can find you.

Make a tiny hole here

Draw yourself here

Paul is not here with you now, though, is he?

No. He was taken to Rome—but I have much to do, so I stayed here.

What do you do?

You're not a cook, by any chance, are you? My tummy's rumbling.

Well, most of my time is spent teaching people about Jesus. You see, God has shown me that he wants me to keep on working for the faith that Jesus taught us.

> Timothy, my child, I entrust to you this command, which is in accordance with the words of prophecy spoken in the past about you. Keep your faith and a clear conscience.
>
> 1 Timothy 1:18

That's what it says in this letter from Paul—is this from the book that you spoke of before?

Yes, the Bible.

You mean the book...

Oh, I see. But for us the Bible is THE book, the most important of all books.

No, the Bible...

But 'bible' and 'book' mean the same thing!

... and I'm in it?

Yes—your name appears lots of times.

44

How many times is Timothy's name hidden in this puzzle? The answer is hidden on the diary page.

```
T I M O T H Y T I O T T M
I I M T I M O T H Y T M O
M T M T M I T I M O T H Y
O Y T O O T I M O T H Y M
T I M O T H Y O Y H T H T
H T O Y H H M T I M H M O
Y T I M Y T Y H T I M T Y
I T I M O T H Y T T O H T
```

So you see, I'm here working with the people of God who follow Jesus Christ because they believe that he is the Son of God.

As they were listening to Timothy there was a lot of noise outside the house. Tempo jumped up and started to bark very loudly. Timothy went to see what was going on. He came back with another letter.

Is that another letter?

I bet it's 2 Timothy, like in our Bible.

It's a letter from Paul. He says lots of things... I shall have to get ready and go. Excuse me.

Before the Livewires could say 'Boot', Timothy had hurried away.

Where's he gone?

He's read something in the letter... listen...

Do your best to come to me soon. Only Luke is with me. Get Mark and bring him with you, because he can help me in the work. I sent Tychicus to Ephesus. When you come, bring my coat that I left in Troas with Carpus; bring the books too.

So, my name is in the Bible too! I didn't want to tell you myself... but I did know.

2 Timothy 4:9

Of course!

So he's off to see Paul.

Can we get to Paul?

Which boat does Timothy catch to get to Paul? (Remember he has to go to Troas to get the coat.)

ROME   TROAS   1 2 3 4

45

DIARY

SUNDAY
How many 'Timothys' did you count in the wordsearch? The answer is hidden on this page!

MONDAY
Write a letter to a friend telling them what you have learnt about God.

TUESDAY
Who gets the most letters in your home?

WEDNESDAY
Who would you like to go on a journey with?

THURSDAY
Can you find the letters to Timothy in the Bible?

FRIDAY
What other ways are there of sending messages? Boot likes E-mail best!

SATURDAY

> Father, help us to understand your messages to us no matter how they are sent. Amen.

It's a pity Timothy had to go so soon.

I'd have liked to have found out more about Paul—it sounds like he had an exciting time.

Well, let's find out for ourselves, I'll type into Boot…

46

There are 10 'Timothys'

Well done, Boot! Where are we now?

In the church at Antioch there were some prophets and teachers. The Holy Spirit said to them, "Set apart for me Barnabas and Saul, to do the work to which I have called them."

Acts 13:1

The Livewires didn't know who Saul was. Tim thought that Boot had got a bit mixed up!

Boot flashed up 'Subject Search' on his screen. Annie-log typed 'Saul' and...

Saul was the name that Paul's family used for him. C'mon, Boot.

'Saul' is a Jewish name. That name was given to Paul when he was born as a member of a Jewish family. 'Paul' is a Roman name and was given to him as an official name to show that he was a Roman citizen. Roman citizens had special rights in New Testament times.

It's a good job that we have that encyclopaedia disk!

So Paul had two names because he was a Jew and a Roman.

The Livewires have found out Paul was chosen by God to do a special thing. Do you remember Aaron, Deborah and Daniel? Can you match them to the special thing that they did?

Led Israel in the desert

Won a battle

Told the meaning of dreams

Deborah

Daniel

Aaron

47

What did the Holy Spirit do with Barnabas and Saul then?

Barnabas and Saul sailed to the island of Cyprus.

I went on holiday to Cyprus!

What happened there?

Acts 13:4

Well...

We're not asking you, Tim!

There was a magician who kept on telling the wrong things about God.

Like those magicians that Daniel knew!

Cyprus is an island west of Jerusalem. You could try to find it in an atlas.

Which way is west from your home?

Why don't you make a compass and find out?

Making a compass is easy...

If you buy a bar magnet you can make a compass by floating it on water. Keep it away from metal things and let it float freely on something light like a meat tray.

If you want to make a compass with a point you can magnetize a needle and then float it on a thin slice of cork. (Get a grown-up to cut the cork because it doesn't cut easily.)

You magnetize the needle by rubbing an ordinary magnet along it, always in the same direction...

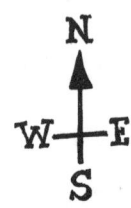

Where did Paul go next?

That was Acts 13—let's try Acts 14.

We are here to announce the Good News, to turn you to the living God who made heaven, earth, sea and all that is in them.

That's not where he is—it's what he is doing!

He's in a town called Lystra.

Hey, Timothy told us about Lystra—that's where he met Paul!

You have to cross the sea to get there...

Acts 14:15

BOOOT!!

Boot had whizzed them all to Lystra—without being asked, too! They landed at the edge of a crowd, who were listening to Paul!

We are here to announce the Good News, to turn you to the living God who made heaven, earth, sea and all that is in them.

Paul finished speaking and walked away, past the Livewires. Little Ben touched his arm.

Excuse me, but what do you mean by ...to turn to the living God...?

Yeah, all this turning around is making me dizzy!

Paul told them that he had been sent by Jesus' disciples to tell people all around the world about the great things that Jesus had done.

What do you think Paul means by '...turn you to the living God...' ?

Write your answer in the compass.

49

Dear Lord, it is very easy in our confusing world to spin round and round, not knowing which way to go. Train us to face the right way and to follow in your track.

God has always given evidence of his existence by the good things he does: he gives you rain from heaven and crops at the right times; he gives you food and fills your hearts with happiness. Let me tell you about the time he helped me and my friend Silas when we were in prison.

We know this story, Timothy told it to us.

But Timothy had not told the Livewires what had happened inside the jail. And now here they were hearing the story from Paul himself.

The jailer called for a light, rushed in, and fell trembling at the feet of Paul and Silas. Then he led them out and asked, "Sirs, what must I do to be saved?" They answered, "Believe in the Lord Jesus."

Acts 16:29

I don't understand, what did the jailer have to be saved from?

I don't think it was really a 'from'—it was more sort of a turning the right way.

Saved from going down the wrong path...

And then being trained to go in the right direction.

Finding the right direction can be difficult. How might you find the right way if you were planning a journey? What would you take with you?

Make a list on this compass.

50

I don't understand. How can we all be going in the wrong direction? If God is everywhere we can't go wrong.

We go wrong when we ignore God. And I think we can try to find God in the wrong places.

You're getting the idea. We need a guide to where God is, just like a compass or a map can guide us.

I get it! The compass uses the earth to point its needle in the right direction, and that is a bit like the earth telling us things...

So... we need to look for God telling us things...

Yeah, and Paul is telling people where not to look.

```
"Since we are God's children, we should
not suppose that his nature is anything
like an image of gold or silver or stone,
shaped by human art and skill."
```

Acts 17:29

The Livewires spun round, pleased that Boot had found what Paul had said about God.

Hey! Where has Paul gone?

Your magnet points from north to south, but how do you know which is which?

Did you have to use another compass to help you?

This is a bit like the people Paul was talking to. They knew that they had to look somewhere and Paul was guiding them in the right direction.

51

Paul had gone to a town called Corinth. Boot knew this and it wasn't long before the Livewires were there as well.

It didn't take Tempo long to sniff Paul out.

Who needs a compass when you have a nose like mine?

Paul was not looking too happy.

What's wrong, Paul?

I don't know. I try and try, but however hard I work there are still so many people who will not believe in Jesus.

You know, we have been all over the place and seen lots of people that God has chosen to train his people — but you can't train them all by yourself!

No, Aaron couldn't do it alone...

...nor could Gideon...

You make me happy by saying that. Do you know that God himself came to me in a dream to tell me that I was not alone? He said...

"Do not be afraid, but keep on speaking and do not give up, for I am with you. No one will be able to harm you, for many in this city are my people."

Acts 18: 9-10

Dear God, be with us when we feel alone and help us to remember that there are always others who will be with us and help us. Amen.

DIARY

SUNDAY
Have you got any things that you have brought back from journeys?

MONDAY
What do you think is the good news that Paul was speaking of?

TUESDAY
What did you decide 'turn you to the living God' means?

WEDNESDAY
What was your favourite journey?

THURSDAY
Where would you most like to travel to?

FRIDAY
Where would you least like to go?

SATURDAY
Write a prayer for a journey. Here's one you could use if you get stuck.

> **Dear Lord, keep us safe on our travels and be with us as we travel and when we arrive. Amen.**

Hey, where's Paul gone now?

He's harder to keep up with than Tempo!

The Livewires were tired. They decided to find Paul later... and settled down for a nap...

53

The Livewires woke up feeling much better. Annie-log looked around.

Boot, where is Paul?

At this time there was serious trouble in Ephesus because of the Way of the Lord.

Where is Ephesus? I can't keep up with this!

If we are still in Corinth then Ephesus is east of here— across the sea.

Acts 19:23

Tychi gave a loud squeak, landed on Boot's keyboard and whoosh... the Livewires were whirled into Boot's disk drive.

WHOOSH

They landed with lots of noise, but no one in Ephesus noticed —they were too busy making a noise themselves!

What is all that racket?

They were in a very busy place—full of people shouting. A man was trying to speak to the crowd, but they just kept on shouting...

Great is Artemis of Ephesus!

They sound like a football crowd.

And who is Artemis?

Tempo did not like it at all. Suddenly he began to bark...

I can smell someone I know.

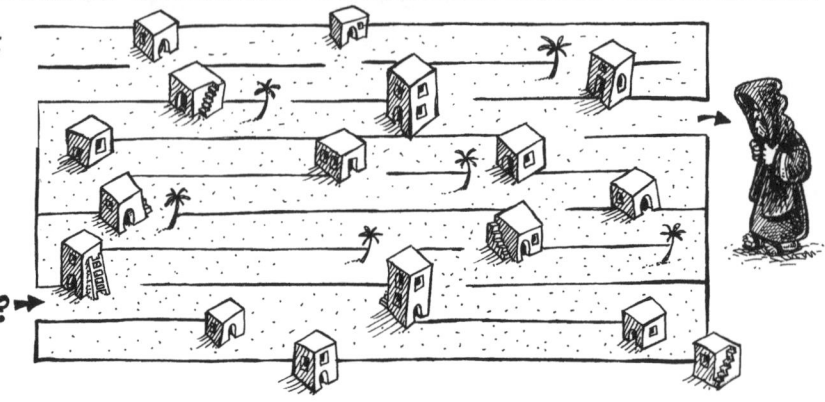

The Livewires followed Tempo and he led them through the streets of Ephesus.

54

Can you guess who he led them to?

Suddenly, there before them was Paul, looking very tired. He looked up as they arrived. It was evening now and getting dark.

Oh, it's you again. I've had terrible trouble. There's a temple in this town which is used to worship a goddess called Artemis. Once the people started to believe in Jesus they stopped buying things to worship Artemis with. The Greeks who sold the things got very cross 'cos they weren't making any money. There was a big riot.

We know, we found it.

There were footsteps behind them and a figure came out of the shadows. The Livewires were worried that it might be someone from the riot...

It's all right, this is my friend Alexander.

It's over, Paul, the people have all gone home. The town clerk came and told them that we had done nothing really wrong...

Well, we hadn't! But it just goes to show what can happen when you start to tell people about Jesus. So many people take it the wrong way.

It's easy to misunderstand sometimes. Think of all the words that mean two things. Can you link the words below to their meanings? All of them have two...

FINE   TRAIN   CROSS   BOX

good weather   a container

practise a game   angry

two pieces of wood joined in the middle

fight   money taken as a punishment

a form of transport

Can you think of any others?

55

Paul said goodbye to the Livewires...

You have travelled a long way.

I'm sorry, I must go now. I'm going to speak to the followers of Jesus before I go on to my next town.

As Paul spoke, Digit drew little maps so that he would not forget...

Yes, I've made three journeys now. I have spent many years travelling around. I went to Cyprus first, then to...

The first journey from Perga to Lystra and Derbe
- Perga, Lystra, Derbe, Cyprus

The second journey from Antioch to Troas, Philippi and Athens and Jerusalem
- Philippi, Troas, Athens, Jerusalem, Antioch

The third journey from Antioch to Corinth and Ephesus
- Ephesus, Corinth, Antioch

...and now I think that I should be going back towards Jerusalem.

Paul left them and walked off into the moonlight.

He reminds me of Daniel, facing problems far from home, yet staying faithful to God...

...and dreaming.

These trainers have to work very hard. I wonder if Paul had a rest when he got to Jerusalem?

Let's find out!!

She rushed to Boot and typed... Boot didn't make them wait long before whoosh... they were on their way.

56 Can you join up the dots on the maps Digit has drawn to show the route Paul took on his three journeys? You could use a different colour crayon for each journey.

They stood outside the temple and were suddenly surprised by the sound of shouting and yelling. There in front of them on the steps of the temple was Paul—surrounded by guards. He had been arrested!

The Livewires followed Paul, at a distance. He was taken before the council of the Jews and they decided to send Paul to see the Roman Governor.

"Where...?"

"In a town called Caesarea—it's by the coast. Ready, Boot?"

Boot did not reply. The Livewires were caught up in a swirl and they landed, untidily, in a courtyard. Paul was standing in front of the governor. They could not hear what the governor was saying, but Boot gave a beep and his words appeared on the screen.

He asked Paul, "Would you be willing to go to Jerusalem and be tried there?" Paul said, "I am standing before the Emperor's own court. I have done no wrong. I appeal to the Emperor!"

Acts 25:9

The crowd around the courtyard went quiet. The governor had no choice, Paul was a Roman citizen and he was allowed to ask to go to the Emperor if he wished...

"That means another journey!"

"Which way is Rome?"

"North west, across the sea."

It took a while for a boat to be got ready. The Livewires were not sure that they wanted to try to follow Paul...

"I hate boats!"

What do you think the Livewires prayed before they set off?

The Livewires were not sure about this trip and were even less happy when they heard Paul talking to the captain...

> I see that our voyage from here will be dangerous. There will be great damage to the cargo and to the ship...

The captain did not think that there would be a storm so they all set off to go to Rome. There was a great storm, just as Paul said. As they sailed along the coast of Crete the wind rose and blew from the north-east. The waves grew huge and everyone was frightened for their lives.

The storm went on for two weeks. The little ship was blown miles beyond Crete until no one knew where they were. Finally, during the night the sailors found that the water was getting shallower and shallower—they must be near land.

> Great! We're going to be able to land. Hooray!

> I hope so—please say that we land, Boot!

Acts 27:39

When day came, the sailors did not recognize the coast, but they noticed a bay with a beach and decided that, if possible, they would run the ship aground there.

> But the ship hit a sandbank and went aground; the front part of the ship got stuck and could not move, while the back part was being broken to pieces by the violence of the waves.

> Oh no!! Whoooaah!

Acts 27:41

The Livewires were thrown to the deck as the boat hit the sandbank.

The island is a place that Paul hasn't been to yet. Can you find it in this line of place names? (Paul has been to all but one.)

EPHESUSPHILIPPIMALTAPERGAJERUSALEMANTIOCHLYSTRADERBE

58 To help you, here is a list of the places Paul has been: Ephesus, Perga, Lystra, Berea, Philippi, Corinth, Jerusalem, Antioch, Derbe.

No one knew which island they had arrived at (except you of course!) but they all jumped off into the water and held on to bits of the wrecked boat...

Boot! Help!

Little Ben couldn't swim!!

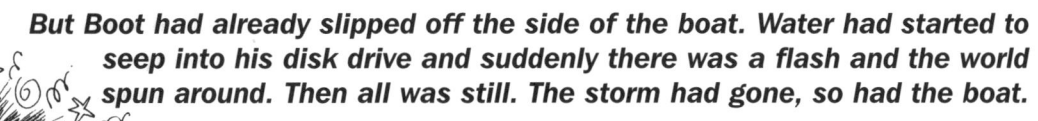

But Boot had already slipped off the side of the boat. Water had started to seep into his disk drive and suddenly there was a flash and the world spun around. Then all was still. The storm had gone, so had the boat.

But the Livewires were still in the water!

Boot couldn't swim.

Tychi could swim. She towed Boot towards the shore. Little Ben held on to Boot's upturned rollerblades.

They got to the shore easily, it was so calm now.

Tychi had some bad news.

Boot will be able to talk to us, but we are stuck here until his disk drive dries out!

Annie-log went over to Boot and typed 'Paul'.

```
After three months we sailed away on a
ship from Alexandria which had spent
the winter in the island. When we arrived
in Rome, Paul was allowed to live by
himself with a soldier guarding him.
```

Acts 28: 11 & 16

The Livewires were worried about Paul...

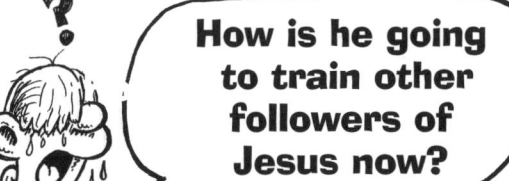

How is he going to train other followers of Jesus now?

Can you guess what Paul will do?

Dear Father, thank you for all the trainers that you have given to us, for Paul and Timothy, Daniel and Aaron and all those who have told us about you throughout history.

SUNDAY
Do you like boats?

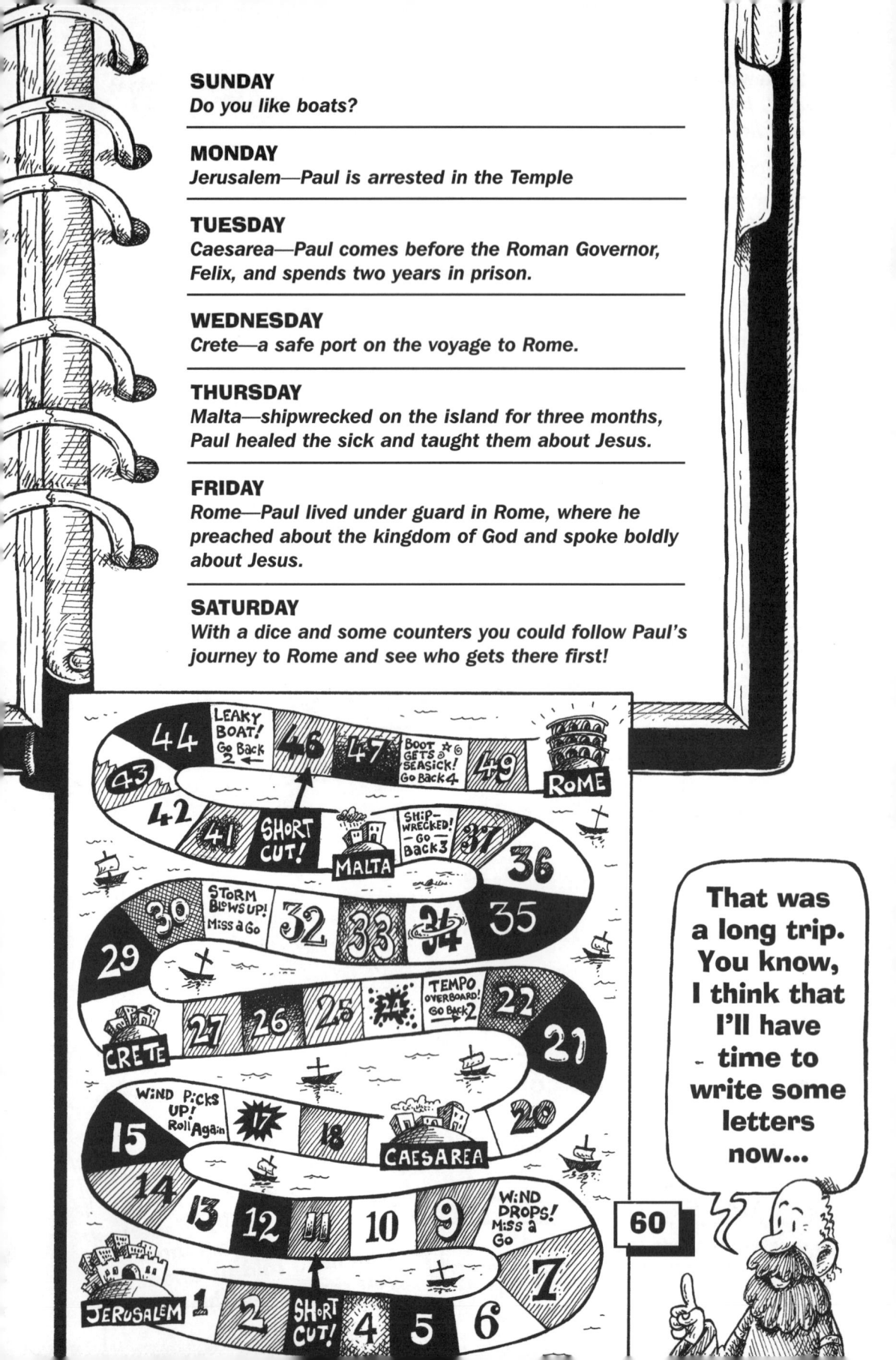

MONDAY
Jerusalem—Paul is arrested in the Temple

TUESDAY
Caesarea—Paul comes before the Roman Governor, Felix, and spends two years in prison.

WEDNESDAY
Crete—a safe port on the voyage to Rome.

THURSDAY
Malta—shipwrecked on the island for three months, Paul healed the sick and taught them about Jesus.

FRIDAY
Rome—Paul lived under guard in Rome, where he preached about the kingdom of God and spoke boldly about Jesus.

SATURDAY
With a dice and some counters you could follow Paul's journey to Rome and see who gets there first!

That was a long trip. You know, I think that I'll have time to write some letters now...

The Livewires decided to explore while they were waiting for Boot's disk drive to dry out. They walked a little way into the island, to the top of a little hill. They were all looking west...

There are some big clouds there, I think...

...it's going to...

RAIN!

Boot was still not quite better, but at least he knew why it was raining...

> He gives you rain from heaven and crops at the right times; he gives you food and fills your hearts with happiness.
>
> Acts 14:17

Who gives us rain?

God, of course!

The Livewires were a bit puzzled because they knew that they were not always happy.

Well, when I am happy I can say 'thank you' to God for that...

Yeah, because his world is so good.

But what about all the unhappy people with no food and things like that?

Like the refugees that Aaron was with.

Data was puzzled by this, but Tim explained that this was the bit that she had missed when she had got left behind...

So our job is to help other people whenever we can so that they can be happy.

And to do what we can to help the unhappy people. We can tell them about God, too—then we'll be real trainers!

What could you do to be a trainer for God? Write it in the compass.

The Livewires looked north this time. They could see where a river came from and the twisting path it took between the trees.

GOT IT!

What?

Well, you see how the river knows which path to take through the trees? Well, God made the world for all of us to live in. He has shown us how he wants us to take care of it. If it gets into a mess—like Digit's bedroom—then we won't be able to live in it! Things need their proper places, like the river and the trees.

I see. So living in the world means that sometimes you have to do jobs to keep it clean and tidy—a bit like washing up at home.

Boot made a sort of growling noise and then went quiet. The Livewires looked at him in astonishment.

Yeah, but the world is clever isn't it? If we don't mess it up it can look after itself...

That's all very well, but we do mess it up—I'm not quite sure what to do about it...

Annie-log tried to get some help from Boot. He seemed to respond, but then gave a little jump, made a sudden loud noise and then shut down.

Let me try, I think he's caught a chill... Got it!

Our Father in heaven: May your holy name be honoured; may your Kingdom come; may your will be done on earth as it is in heaven.

Matthew 6:9-10

I know that, it's the Lord's Prayer—we did it at school.

62

How could you help to care for God's world? Make a list on the compass.